Jesus in the
Seven Feasts
Of Israel

Any inquiries or comments about the content of this
book should be directed to:

Rock of Israel Ministries
P.O. Box 18038
Fairfield, OH 45018
513-874-2566

www.rockofisrael.org
info@rockofisrael.org

All scriptures are taken from *The Holy Bible, New
King James Version*, (Nashville, Tennessee: Thomas
Nelson, Inc.) 1982.

Table of Contents

Forward

My son Doug, a devoted husband, father, and son, speaks from the bottom of his heart. The years have come and gone, and what he believes in still lives on. He has poured out his heart and soul to many who have heard him. He also traveled all over, near and far.

Over the years he has studied much. He has now combined all his thoughts and written this book, which was his goal, to express what he has learned by being a believer.

I hope that when you come to the last page of this book, you will understand why I am the proud grandmother of his five children and proud to have him for a son.

Marcia W.
Middletown, New York

Introduction

There's a humorous story told about three rabbis who have a problem with mice in their synagogue. The first rabbi explains, "We called the best exterminator in town, and he couldn't get them to leave." Then the second rabbi exclaims, "We had the same thing happen to us. We got the best pest control person in town to come over, and he couldn't get them to leave either!" Finally, the last rabbi says, "Well, we got rid of them all, and it was pretty simple if you ask me. All we did was make them little yarmulkes and gave them little Bar-Mitzvahs and we haven't seen them since!"

While this story is cute, it also represents an unfortunate trend in modern Jewish society today. Most Jewish people are ignorant of their own Jewish Scriptures. The vast majority of Jewish youth today attend synagogue before age 13 for the sole purpose of preparing for their Bar-Mitzvah. Once that event is accomplished, there really is very little synagogue attendance or reading of the Hebrew Scriptures (what we commonly call the "Old Testament") for them.

Up until 1986, I was one of those typical Jewish youths as well. I was Bar-Mitzvah at the age of 13 (in 1977) and that was the last time I attended synagogue on a regular weekly basis. Of course I was still in synagogue for all the important annual Jewish High Holiday Day services.

A Bar Mitzvah today

However, I knew nothing of the Jewish Scriptures, which should be the lifeblood of every Jewish person. How thankful I am that since becoming a believer in 1986, I have devoured the Old Testament again and again. I love to read it, and I love to teach on it. Why? Because I see Jesus throughout the Book.

When talking to Jewish people one day, Jesus said, "For if you believed Moses, you would believe Me; for he wrote about Me." (John 5:46) Moses wrote the Torah (Genesis – Deuteronomy). How is Jesus in those books? One of the ways is by looking at the 'types and shadows' there.

It's my prayer that as you read this book, you will be illuminated to see the original Seven Feasts of Israel in all their glory and then to see the Messiah of Israel – Jesus – in all His glory as the fulfillment of each of those feasts. May God bless you as you begin this new journey.

<u>The Feast of Passover</u>

'These are the feasts of the LORD, holy convocations
which you shall proclaim at their appointed times.
'On the fourteenth day of the first month at twilight is
the LORD's Passover.

Leviticus chapter 23: verses 4-5

The first of the seven annual Feasts of the Lord is
Passover. Hardly a person over 40 years old has not
seen the epic movie production by Cecil B. DeMille
called "The Ten Commandments." In this blockbuster
classic, Charlton Heston (Moses) and Yule Brenner
(Pharaoh) go head-to-head with each other for Israel's
freedom. Pharaohs' power becomes less and less, and
Moses' power becomes more and more. Of course the
movie ends with the famous crossing of the Red Sea
and Israel receiving the Ten Commandments by the
hand of Moses. It was a very great movie in its time.

Above all else, we need to remember that although
Hollywood has taken much liberty with the story, the
event of Passover is a historical event. It is an event
that happened in space/time history in a land called
Egypt and a continent called Africa. Let's briefly
review what happened about 3,500 years ago.

Israel had been in Egypt for 430 years. At first, the
trip there seemed like a good idea. There had been a

famine, so Jacob and his entire family went down to Egypt because – as a surprise to him - his son Joseph had become the second in power only behind Pharaoh himself.

Joseph sold into slavery by his brothers.
He eventually became a leader in Egypt

Joseph had instituted a wonderful food program in Egypt, so a trip there made perfect sense at the time. If you don't know the whole story, I highly suggest you read it in Genesis 37-48. It's one of my favorites.

After many years had passed, a new pharaoh came on the scene (who knew not of Joseph), and the scenario changed for Israel...

Exodus 1:8-11
Now there arose a new king over Egypt, who did not know Joseph. And he said to his people, "Look, the people of the children of Israel are more and mightier than we; "come, let us deal shrewdly with them, lest

*they multiply, and it happen, in the event of war,
that they also join our enemies and fight against us,
and so go up out of the land." Therefore they set
taskmasters over them to afflict them with their
burdens. And they built for Pharaoh supply cities,
Pithom and Raamses.*

Isn't life a lot like that sometimes? We start out with
the best of plans and then end up in slavery in a place
we don't want to be. But thankfully the story does not
end there. It was just the beginning for Israel.
Somewhere in Egypt one day, an Israelite
woman gave birth to a very special baby boy.

Although forced infanticide was the will of the
Pharaoh for newborn Israelite boys, this woman was
not afraid of the king's edict and hid her newborn son
for several months. Eventually, she could not hide the
boy any longer, so she put him in a basket on the Nile
River and sent big sister Miriam to watch over him
from a distance. The Pharaoh's daughter, at the Nile
River that morning, finds him there and names him
"Drawn out" (or, as we would say in English today,
"Moses").

Baby Moses finds a new home

To top it off, Miriam suggests to Pharaoh's daughter that she knows a Hebrew woman who could nurse the baby for her. It seemed like a good idea to Pharaoh's daughter and so baby Moses gets his mother back for the time being.

Eventually, Moses was raised in all the wisdom of Egypt, however at some point in time, Moses discovers that he is a Hebrew too. One day he has a choice to make. An Egyptian was beating a Hebrew slave right in front of him so Moses kills the Egyptian. The next day, trying to break up a fight between two Hebrews, they basically say to him, "Stay out of this. Who made you a ruler over us? You helped us by killing that Egyptian yesterday and now you think you're our King and Ruler?!" (My paraphrase of Exodus 2:14)

Obviously Egyptian news had covered the story, and Moses knew that this would not sit too kindly with Pharaoh. So Moses decides to pack his bags and take the first Greyhound bus out of Egypt and go to the land of Midian.

But this was all in God's plan. Moses thought that he could deliver Israel by his own muscle, but they rejected him. Ever feel like that? You only wanted to help but somehow seem to make things worse? Moses then spent the next 40 years away from his people, until one day he met God. You remember the famous

burning bush encounter. God tells him that he
(Moses) is going to return to Egypt to help his people
- only this time God will be with him. Reluctantly,
Moses agrees and finds his way into Pharaoh's court,
announcing God's desire to free Israel so that they can
worship Him.

Pharaoh says 'no way' and turns the heat up on Israel's
slavery a notch or two. Go get your own straw for
bricks... Keep the same number of bricks coming...
yada, yada, yada. The reader of the text knows that
Pharaoh's days are numbered - only Pharaoh does not
realize it yet. You cannot go up against God and win.
The Israelites apparently don't realize this either.
They even get pretty 'ticked' with Moses at this point.
Ever felt like that? "God, I prayed for help, and things
only seem to be getting worse." Hang on; thankfully
the story does not end here.

Nine plagues later, Egypt's economy is in shambles.
Egypt's gods are wobbling. But Pharaoh still refuses
to let them go. Now, he has offered Moses a few
compromises along the way, like 'Go, but leave the
children behind' or 'Go, but don't go far', but Moses
won't take anything less than 100%. I'll never forget
the first night God woke me up to my spiritual
condition in May of 1986. I felt the conviction over
my sins big time, and at 2:30 in the morning I began to
make deals with God. "Ok, God, I'll cut this out 25%
and that out 50%, etc."

16

I had no peace that night until I gave God 100% of what He wanted. God's kind of funny like that. He likes to get His way all the time. (And thankfully so!)

The ominous tenth plague is about to strike. Remember what Egypt did to the Hebrew baby boys? Well, the old statement, "What goes around, comes around," is surely a biblical principle. To put it in the words of scripture, *"God is not mocked; for whatever a man sows, that he will also reap."* (Galatians 6:7) To put it in my own words, Egypt will get a taste of their own medicine.

Exodus 11:4-7
Then Moses said, "Thus says the LORD: 'About midnight I will go out into the midst of Egypt; 'and all the firstborn in the land of Egypt shall die, from the firstborn of Pharaoh who sits on his throne, even to the firstborn of the female servant who is behind the handmill, and all the firstborn of the animals. 'Then there shall be a great cry throughout all the land of Egypt, such as was not like it before, nor shall be like it again. 'But against none of the children of Israel shall a dog move its tongue, against man or beast, that you may know that the LORD does make a difference between the Egyptians and Israel.'

All of Egypt will be devastated by this plague. Not a home will be without a dead person in it. But God tells Moses that the Israelites should do something very specific to 'protect' themselves from this last plague of death. Each family should (or, if they needed, several small families could combine) separate out a one-year-old male lamb from their flock. Examine it for four days. Make sure that it has no spot or blemish. It must be a perfect lamb. On the 14th day of the lunar month, the lamb was to be slain. The lambs' blood was to be placed on the doorposts of their home - the top and sides of the door.

The blood of the Lamb

It was applied with hyssop and probably applied by the patriarch of the family. The lamb itself was then to be brought into the home, and it was to be roasted over a fire that evening. The meal was also to consist of bitter herbs and bread made without yeast (see Exodus 12:8). Thus we have the first *Seder* meal. (Incidentally, the Seder meal is the meal today that the Jewish people eat each year on that anniversary date of Passover to commemorate what God did for them many years ago that night in Egypt.)

Since it was a full moon (the 14th day of the lunar month), what was done to the doorposts that evening could be seen by all in the community. There were no 'secret' believers in Egypt that night. No one could hide his or her affiliation under that full moon. Either there was lambs' blood on your doorposts or there wasn't. It was that simple. At midnight, the destroyer began his journey. Many people believe that it was death itself that "passed over" the homes of the Israelites that evening, but actually the scripture tells us it was the Lord who "passed over" each home with the lambs' blood on it. The purpose of His passing over was to protect that family, "*and when I see the blood, I will pass over you...*" (Ex 12:13). In other words, God Himself "passed over" (i.e. stopped) at the home and kept death from entering in. The same word, "Passover" (in Hebrew, "Pesach"), is used of the Lord "passing over" Jerusalem to protect it like a mother bird. *"Like birds flying about, so will the LORD of hosts defend Jerusalem. Defending, He will also deliver it; **Passing over**, He will preserve it."* (Isaiah 31:5).

So do you get the picture yet? Egypt kills Israel's children. God is now going to return the favor upon the land of Egypt. However, His gracious provision for Israel was to show them that blood had already been shed at their home. A substitute had died for their firstborn. A lamb was slain.

Now let's move forward in time to the first century -
the time period of Jesus. The city is Jerusalem. The
ones now oppressing the Israelites are not Egyptians,
but Romans. Many people are hearing of this itinerant
Jewish preacher from the Galilee area who works
miracles. The word on the streets is that He is arriving
in Jerusalem today. Wait, here he is! Riding on a
donkey of all things? What does it matter! God
delivered us once from the Egyptians, and it looks like
He will finally do it again, but this time from the
Romans! Let's welcome him! Hosanna! Here he
comes. Spread the palm branches. He will surely
save us from the Romans.

Alfred Edersheim describes the scene:

> We can imagine it all – how the fire would leap
> from heart to heart. So He was the promised
> Son of David – and the Kingdom was at hand!
> It may have been just as the precise point of the
> road was reached, where 'the City of David'
> first suddenly emerges into view, 'at the descent
> of the Mount of Olives,' that the whole
> multitude of the disciples began to rejoice and
> praise God with a loud voice for all the mighty
> works that they had seen'. As the burning words
> of joy and praise, the record of what they had
> seen, passed from mouth to mouth, and they
> caught sight of 'the City of David,' adorned as a
> bride to welcome her King – Davidic praise to
> David's Greater Son wakened the echoes of old

Davidic Psalms in the morning-light of their fulfillment."1

Here we have Jesus coming into Jerusalem several days before the Passover. He uses His time in the city wisely - teaching and confronting the religious leadership. The city population has swelled that week because of the Jewish people arriving to celebrate the Jewish deliverance of Passover. The lambs will be slaughtered in a few days.

The timing could not have been worse for the Temple leadership as author J. Dwight Pentecost explains,

"The Jewish leaders saw the Passover as an opportune time to put Jesus to death. They reasoned that if Israel accepted Jesus as Messiah and He instituted a kingdom, Rome would move in and destroy this rival kingdom. It seemed better to the Jewish leaders that one man should die that the whole nation should perish at the hands of Rome."2

The day of the Passover is near. Israel has been celebrating an anniversary Seder meal every Passover to remember what God did for them in Egypt centuries ago. Jesus and His disciples are going to celebrate that meal too. However, Jesus takes some of the key elements of the Seder meal and infuses them with new meaning. The unleavened bread He uses as a remembrance for His body and the fruit of the vine He uses as a remembrance of His blood.

That night in Israel, thousands of Seders will be going on and fathers will tell their children about the body and the blood of that little spotless lamb from centuries ago. Jesus tells His disciples to begin to remember Him from now on. He is the Lamb.

After the Seder meal, Jesus goes to a garden across from the city to pray. Of course, earlier that evening, Jesus was betrayed. The soldiers now arrive and arrest Him. All His disciples flee. After a series of short "trials," He is beaten and taken out by Roman soldiers to be publicly executed on a cross with three nails. Of course blood is coming from all over Him due to the beatings by the Romans, but the key thing to notice is where the nails are placed. A nail on the left wrist, one on the right wrist, one on the feet, and a crown of thorns on His head.

Look at the position of the blood coming from Him. Left, right, top, and bottom. It's the same 'spots' as the little lambs' blood on the doorposts in Egypt many years ago. In Egypt, there was no blood put on the floor (probably out of respect - so as to not step on the blood), but most certainly some would have dripped down from the top, forming a cross at the family's front door, sealing them and protecting them from judgment.

Don't you see it? In Egypt, there was nothing that would have protected the family except the lambs' blood. No amount of praying or giving of charity or anything else would have kept them safe. It was only the lambs' blood that saved them from judgment that night. The same thing holds true today. It was said of Jesus, *"Behold! The Lamb of God who takes away the sin of the world!"* John 1:29. That means being religious does not save a person from their sins. No amount of charity, no amount of praying, saves a person. What saves a man from their sins is - when a simple but profound act of faith takes place.

When you ask the Lamb of God into your heart. When He comes in and places His own blood upon the doorposts of your heart. It is then - and only then - that you are 'saved' from God's judgment.

I remember as a child that our family would get together in upstate NY for Seder dinners. At the Seder each year, a child is supposed to read "The Four Questions," which help to better explain the Passover to children. One year I was told that it was going to be my turn to read them. For several weeks, I practiced them over and over again until I got them right and fully memorized them. At the Seder meal we recalled the story of Passover and sang songs about our deliverance from Egypt. However, it was all so distant. No talk about a current relationship with the God who delivered us from Egypt. No talk about a God who delivers us today in our daily lives.

Encarta Encyclopedia, Leland Bobbe/Tony Stone Images

A Modern Passover Seder

Today, as a believer, I can say that I really do know personally the same God who delivered Israel 3,500 years ago. For almost four decades now, I can rejoice that I am free from the judgment of sin due to me because of the blood of the spotless Lamb, Jesus, the Jewish Messiah.

And just as Jewish people have a meal called the Seder to help them remember their deliverance from Egypt, so too did Jesus give believers a meal to remember Him as the Lamb of God who delivers us from death. That meal is called Communion.

Thank you, God, for saving me from death. Though it cost You so much, I would be lost without Your blood. Thank you Messiah, for enduring that suffering for me. Thank you from the bottom of my heart.

Endnotes

1) Alfred Edersheim, The Life and Times of Jesus the Messiah (Peabody, Massachusetts: Hendrickson Publishers, 1993), p. 728.
2) J. Dwight Pentecost, The Words and Works of Jesus Christ (Grand Rapids, Michigan: Academie Books / Zondervan Publishing House, 1981), pp. 369-370

The Feast of Unleavened Bread

*'And on the fifteenth day of the same month is the
Feast of Unleavened Bread to the LORD; seven days
you must eat unleavened bread.*

Leviticus chapter 23: verse 6

Deeply associated with the holiday of Passover is the
Feast of Unleavened Bread. Perhaps you have heard
of unleavened bread today by its more common name
- "matzah." And although Passover and Unleavened
Bread have 'merged' in the modern Jewish mindset as
one holiday, biblically they are two distinct events. So
let's take a look at the Feast of Unleavened Bread and
its relationship to Passover.

The Feast of Unleavened Bread is a seven-day event.
It begins on the 15th day of the Jewish month of Nisan
(usually corresponding to our calendar as late March
or early April) and ends on the 21st day of Nisan. Its
origins go back to that very first Passover night in
Egypt. The night when the family had to place the
blood of the lamb on the doorposts of their home.
Then, they were told to go inside, have a meal, and
include unleavened bread as part of that meal.

Exodus 12:8

"Then they shall eat the flesh on that night; roasted in fire, with unleavened bread and with bitter herbs they shall eat it."

Here we have the first Passover Seder. Unleavened bread was one of the three main ingredients of that meal. (Lamb and bitter herbs being the other two.) Leaven (called 'chometz' in Hebrew) means 'sour.' Leaven is the ingredient that makes bread rise. Leaven was not allowed at the table nor anywhere in the home during Passover.

As a matter of fact, the entire household had to be cleansed of any food that would contain even a trace of leaven.

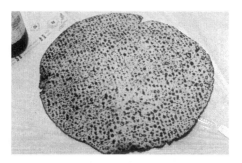

Unleavened Bread

Exodus 13:19

"For seven days no leaven shall be found in your houses, since whoever eats what is leavened, that same person shall be cut off from the congregation of

Israel, whether he is a stranger or a native of the land."

From the night of their redemption from Egypt and for the next seven days, no leaven was to be found anywhere in the home. As the years went by, to make sure that there was no leaven in the homes during this feast, Jewish people would prepare for days and even weeks earlier. Leavened food was physically removed from the premises, and utensils were brought into the kitchen that had never been used on leavened products before. As a matter of fact, a special search is made in the home during the last remaining hours before Passover to make sure that no leaven remains. Alfred Edersheim explains:

> "...on the evening commenced the 14th of Nisan, when a solemn search was made with lighted candle throughout each house for any leaven that might be hidden, or have fallen aside by accident." 1

He continues to explain when the physical ingestion of all leaven stopped:

> "... an hour before midday was fixed, after which nothing leavened might be eaten. The more strict abstained from it even an hour earlier (at 10 o'clock), lest the eleventh hour might insensibly run into the forbidden midday." 2

So we can see that Jewish people took this feast very seriously. Even Jesus made preparations for His Passover dinner by having His disciples make sure the room where they would eat the Passover would be ready in time.

<u>Mark 14:12-16</u>
Now on the first day of Unleavened Bread, when they killed the Passover lamb, His disciples said to Him, "Where do You want us to go and prepare, that You may eat the Passover?"

And He sent out two of His disciples and said to them, "Go into the city, and a man will meet you carrying a pitcher of water; follow him. "Wherever he goes in, say to the master of the house, 'The Teacher says "Where is the guest room in which I may eat the Passover with My disciples?" ' "Then he will show you a large upper room, furnished and prepared; there make ready for us."

So His disciples went out, and came into the city, and found it just as He had said to them; and they prepared the Passover.

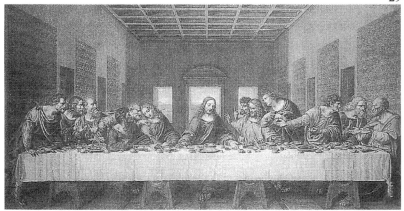

Most do not realize the "Last Supper" was a Passover.
No leavened bread was served.

I still remember growing up in that small apartment in
the Bronx. Before Passover began, my grandmother
would prepare for the holiday by boxing up any food
with leaven in it and placing it in the big closet in the
hallway. I guess that was good enough for her. Out
of sight - out of mind. (The real reason probably
being, I don't think she could financially afford to
simply throw out food.)

One must eventually ask oneself the question of
"Why?" Why is the removal of leaven so important?
What significance does it play in Holy Scripture? Neil
and Jamie Lash give a good summary of the role of
leaven in biblical thought:

> "Leaven, in both Jewish and Christian tradition,
> is *symbolic of sin*. The Talmud sys, "leaven
> represents the evil impulse of the heart"
> (Berachot 17a). We've already seen that

chometz (leaven) literally means, "sour." That's what sin does to our lives. It makes them sour rather than sweet." 3

Moishe Rosen also explains well the role of leaven:

"Leaven in the Bible [with the exception of Matt 13:33] is almost always a symbol of sin. The putting away of all leaven is a picture of the sanctification of the child of God.... In teaching His people this truth, God did not leave them to grapple with abstractions. The Bible speaks in terms of human experience. Leaven was something that every housewife, every cook, used in everyday life. The feel, the smell, and the effects of leaven had obvious meaning.

The Hebrew word for leaven is chometz, meaning "bitter" or "sour." It is the nature of sin to make people bitter or sour. Leaven causes dough to become puffed up so that the end product is more in volume but not more in weight. The sin of pride causes people to be puffed up, to think of themselves as far more than they really are.

The ancient Hebrews used the sourdough method of leavening their bread. Before a housewife formed the dough into loaves ready for baking, she pulled off a chunk of the raw dough and set it aside in a cool, moist place. When it was time to bake another batch of bread, she brought out the reserve lump of dough. She then mixed the old lump into the fresh batch of flour and water to leaven the next loaves, again setting aside a small lump of the newly mixed dough. Each "new generation" of bread was organically linked by the common yeast spores to the previous loaves of bread. The human race bears this same kind of link to the sin nature of our first father, Adam." 4

Today, Judaism denies the existence of what theologians call "original sin." They would ascribe to a theology similar to advice giver Dr. Laura: "just do the right thing." Judaism is a works-based system. If you just try hard enough, you can be a good person. In actuality, isn't that the basis of all world religions?

But the Scriptures teach that mankind has been infected with a virus called sin. And I believe it is transmitted from father to son genetically. This makes every boy and girl born to earthly parents assured to have a sin nature. A 'nature' that will choose wrong (selfish choices) if left to itself. As a father of five, I have never had a problem like, "Come on, girls, you're sharing again! You've always shared. Let me teach you how to be selfish." All parents can attest that what I am saying is true at some point in child rearing. We all need to teach our children *right* behavior. If left to themselves, they would gravitate towards **wrong** behavior.

Incidentally, the reality of this 'sin nature' is why I also believe in the virgin birth of the Messiah. If He had two 'normal' earthly parents, He most certainly would have inherited a sin nature. That is why His heavenly Father arranged it so that His genetics in the womb of Miriam (Mary) would contain no sin nature. A virgin birth did that. He was fully human, but without a propensity to gravitate towards selfish ends.

But I digress; back to Passover and Unleavened Bread. Notice the order? Passover comes first, **and then** the family had seven (the number of completion) days of unleavened bread. In my own life, Jesus saved me in 1986. He came to my heart's door and placed His own blood there protecting me from death. Then He entered into my life and began to remove the leaven. (And did I have lots of leaven!) My desire to gratify 'self' outside of God's will began to die. The leaven began to leave. I no longer wanted to sin. I no longer wanted to live a life of "wine, women, and song."

I think that is what made it so hard for my family to accept. That they had a "new Doug" when they liked the "old Doug."

Rabbi Shaul (the Apostle Paul) told the congregation (the church) at Corinth to stop praising sin. His admonition to them came straight out of this feast:

1 Corinthians 5:6b-8
Do you not know that a little leaven leavens the whole lump? Therefore purge out the old leaven, that you may be a new lump, since you truly are unleavened. For indeed [Messiah], our Passover, was sacrificed for us.

Let us never forget that Jesus is the only one who never sinned. He had no leaven in His life. Even the most righteous of saints has at some point failed. We all need leaven continuously removed from our lives. Some leaven we can see. It's obvious to us and to those around us. Other times, it's something that we cannot see.

Either way, a good prayer by David (and one that I personally pray) is found in Psalm 139:23-24. *"Search me, O God, and know my heart: try me, and know my anxieties: And see if there is any wicked way in me, and lead me in the way everlasting."* Asking God to do the housecleaning is much better than trying to use those 'self-help' books the world depends on. God does a much better job.

And in closing, let me mention one more thing about bread. It's interesting to discover that Jesus was born in a town called 'Bethlehem.' That's actually two

words in Hebrew, "Beth" means "house" and
"Lechem" means "bread." So isn't it fascinating that
the one who is called the "Bread of Life" was born in a
town called "House of Bread"?

Jesus said, in John

6:35 *"I am the bread of life. He who comes to Me
shall never hunger, and he who believes in Me shall
never thirst."* Have you come to eat of Him and His
unleavened nature?

Endnotes

1) Edersheim, Life and Times, p. 805.
2) Ibid., p. 806
3) Neil & Jamie Lash, Jewish Jewels Newsletter
   (Ft. Lauderdale, Florida), March 1994
4) Moishe Rosen, Christ in the Passover (Chicago,
   Illinois: Moody Press, 1978), p. 29

The Feast of Firstfruits

Speak to the children of Israel, and say to them:
'When you come into the land which I give to you, and
reap its harvest, then you shall bring a sheaf of the
firstfruits of your harvest to the priest. 'He shall wave
the sheaf before the LORD, to be accepted on your
behalf; on the day after the Sabbath the priest shall
wave it.

Leviticus chapter 23: verses 10-11

Priorities. I have heard it said that if you want to see
the real spirituality of a person, look at their
checkbook. Of course we all have to pay bills. Of
course God expects us to save some money to take
care of our family. But the issue is - which comes
first? Who (or what) gets 'first dibs' on our money?
Do we give to God and to His Kingdom first or last? I
can hear some of you now, "But we're not under the
law!" True, I never said anything about compulsory
giving. But shouldn't a person who claims to have had
a new birth - a changed heart - show that in some real
and tangible way? And what better way to show it
than by giving a portion of what you have to God?
After all, it's His anyway!

That is some of what the Feast of Firstfruits was all
about. After Passover, Israel was heading towards the

Promised Land. God had already told them that it would be a land flowing with milk and honey. Of course that was a symbolic statement about the abundance of **all** the crops and livestock that God was going to give Israel. The firstfruits offering was supposed to be Israel's way of showing their gratefulness to God for giving them the abundance of produce and livestock. And a way to show their gratefulness for the remaining harvest that was to come. It was a tangible way of showing that God came <u>first</u> in their lives.

But there was more significance regarding this holiday. Firstfruits also indicated that Israel knew there was more to come. The dead seeds that they had placed in the ground weeks ago were now coming up. After the first crops were dedicated to God, the rest of the harvest was still to come for them. What anticipation for the farmer if all the conditions had been right that year. What a bountiful harvest they could look forward to!

A field to be harvested

Let's go back to first century Jerusalem three days before the Feast of Firstfruits. On Friday afternoon, Jesus's lifeless body had been taken down from the cross and was being prepared for burial. The disciple John tells us that it was prepared in accordance with Jewish burial customs at the time. *Then they took the body of Jesus, and bound it in strips of linen with the spices, as the custom of the Jews is to bury.* (John 19:40)

The body could not be buried after sundown Friday, so it was speedily prepared for burial that afternoon with the idea that they would return on Sunday morning, after the Sabbath, to help finish the job. *Now on the first day of the week, very early in the morning, they, and certain other women with them, came to the tomb bringing the spices which they had prepared.* (Luke 24:1).

An empty tomb in Jerusalem today
which many tourists visit.

On the first day of the week, the gospel writers tell us that women arrived at the tomb first. That fact alone should tell skeptics who reject the gospel accounts that they are reading history, because the testimony of a woman was not admissible in court in first-century Israel. So if the writers were really fabricating a story and wanted people to believe it, why would they have the women arrive first?

However, the key thing to notice was that on the very same day in Jerusalem when Israel (through the priesthood) was physically waving to God the first fruits of their field, Jesus became the firstfruits of the resurrection of the dead! He rose up from the tomb on Sunday morning – the exact same day as the Jewish Feast of Firstfruits.

Of course the physical resurrection of Messiah's body from the tomb is the cornerstone of our faith! It's not negotiable. There are many things Christians may amiably disagree on, but this is not one of them. The apostle Paul tells us that unless we believe in our hearts that Jesus was raised from the dead, we cannot be saved. After all, why talk to someone that you believe is still dead? *"that if you confess with your mouth the Lord Jesus and believe in your heart that God has raised Him from the dead, you will be saved."* (Romans 10: 9).

Many times I hear Christian apologists (an apologist is someone who defends the faith) trying to prove the resurrection of Jesus by different means of history. Not that those methods are bad, but they always neglect the Old Testament proof of the resurrection! Israel's prophets predicted that it would happen long before it did.

In one such apologetic book appropriately entitled "Evidence that Demands a Verdict," Josh McDowell devotes no less than 80 pages of scholarly research showing evidence for the resurrection of Jesus. For those willing to put in the time, the evidence is quite compelling.

But, in reference to the Old Testament proof, the Apostle Paul states, *"For I delivered to you first of all that which I also received: that [Messiah] died for our sins according to the Scriptures, and that He was buried, and that He rose again the third day according to the Scriptures,"* (1 Corinthians 15: 3-4). Did you catch those last four words..."*according to the scriptures*"? Paul states that the resurrection of the Messiah was predicted according to the Jewish Scriptures! What we commonly call today the Old Testament. And the Feast of Firstfruits is certainly one area where God taught that the body of what had been previously dead (the seed) could live again. The same is true of the Messiah. His body was planted in the earth and was waved alive again on the third day! (For additional references to resurrection in the Old

Testament, see Psalm 16:10, Isaiah 53:10, and Hosea 6:2.)

The great Jewish author Alfred Edersheim puts it well this way:

> *The importance of all this cannot be adequately expressed in words. A dead Messiah might have been a Teacher and Wonder-worker, and remembered and loved as such. But only a Risen and Living Messiah could be the Savior, the Life, and the Life-Giver - and as such preached to all men. And of this most blessed truth we have the fullest and most unquestionable evidence."1*

According to the Sadducees (who ran the Temple services in Jerusalem), this day of "Firstfruits" always occurred on the "first" day of the week after Passover was over – meaning it was always on a Sunday!

It is very interesting to note that the Hebrew name for this "Firstfruits" day is "Yom Ha' Bikkurim" (Day of the First Fruits) and is derived from the same Hebrew root word as "bekhor" – which means "firstborn." So we see an overarching principle at work here. In the Torah, remember that **the firstborn** of man (and beast) belonged to the LORD (see Numbers 8:17). So this principle is applied to the first fruits that ripen each agricultural season as well.

But getting back to the implications of Messiah's physical resurrection for you and me. Well, to put it simply, if He was the first fruits of the resurrection, what does that imply? It certainly does imply there will be more resurrected, right? Who are the more? You and me! Believers in this very same Messiah. He who conquered death and rose from the grave will also **raise us up** from the dead as well. Let this truth sink down into your **kishkas**! (The Yiddish expression for 'guts').

Messiah rose from the dead

Your worst enemy is death, and because God raised Jesus up from the dead, we also will be bodily raised up from the dead. How's that for a future?

As a matter of fact, Paul devotes a whole section of his letter to the believers in Corinth about the subject of bodily resurrection.

1 Corinthians 15: 12-20

"Now if [Messiah] is preached that He has been raised from the dead, how do some among you say that there is no resurrection of the dead? But if there is no resurrection of the dead, then [Messiah] is not risen. And if [Messiah] is not risen, then our preaching is empty and your faith is also empty. Yes, and we are found false witnesses of God, because we have testified of God that He raised up [Messiah], whom He did not raise up—if in fact the dead do not rise. For if the dead do not rise, then [Messiah] is not risen. And if [Messiah] is not risen, your faith is futile; you are still in your sins! Then also those who have fallen asleep in [Messiah] have perished. If in this life only we have hope in [Messiah], we are of all men the most pitiable. But now [Messiah] is risen from the dead, and has become the firstfruits of those who have fallen asleep."

That last sentence summarizes it all. Messiah is the firstfruits of the resurrection. We as believers, even if we die (sleep), are the rest of the fruits. The resurrection of all believers in Jesus will certainly happen one day. And on that day we will get new bodies that are incorruptible, glorious and will never die.

Now, about the resurrection body, we need to unlearn some things about the afterlife that movies have taught us for years. We will not be ghosts or spirits floating around on clouds forever without bodies. The resurrection body will be a genuine body. *"There is a natural body, and there is a spiritual body"* (1 Corinthians 15:44). A spiritual body does not mean it will be a body you cannot see, but it will be a real body adapted to the use and expression of the spirit. It will not be dominated by fleshly desires (as our natural bodies are now), but it will be a body dominated by spiritual, godly desires. As Herman Hoyt explains:

> *The resurrection body will be exactly the same body that experienced death and was laid away in the grave... If the resurrection body were a new body, that would be an act of creation and not resurrection... The structure will remain the same, but it will not be a body of flesh and blood; it will not be the same kind of flesh; but it will be a body adapted to the new sphere in which it will function, and it will consist of flesh and bone (Luke 24:39), and the flesh will be changed for its new purpose and function (1 Corinthians 15:39).1*

Do you get the picture? Our future resurrection is tied to the past resurrection of the Messiah. He was the firstfruit, and we are the many more fruits to follow. Here's some advice I can give only to believers. Don't get too comfortable in your tombs; you're only renting them until Resurrection Day!

Endnotes

5) Herman A. Hoyt, The End Times (Winona Lake, Indiana: BMH Books, 1969), pp.204-205.

The Feast of Weeks

And you shall count for yourselves from the day after the Sabbath, from the day that you brought the sheaf of the wave offering: seven Sabbaths shall be completed. Count fifty days to the day after the seventh Sabbath; then you shall offer a new grain offering to the LORD.

Leviticus chapter 23: verses 15-16

Many Jewish holidays on the calendar are connected with a historical event. Passover is connected with the Exodus, dated about 1450 B.C. Purim celebrates the deliverance of the Jewish people from Haman in the book of Esther about 480 B.C.. Hanukkah is connected with the Maccabee family fighting back the Syrian army and re-dedicating (or "Hanukkah-ing") the Temple in Jerusalem about 165 B.C. The theme of most of these holidays today is "They tried to destroy us. God saved us. Let's eat!" However, this holiday, the Feast of Weeks, is not technically associated with any miracle or historical event, per se. But the time to determine it is definitely connected with Passover.

In Leviticus 23, God tells Israel to count off seven Sabbaths (seven weeks) beginning with the first Sabbath after Passover. So we have a total of 49 days. (Seven days in a week times seven weeks is 49 days.)

Then, on the 50th day, several things were to happen. One thing was the waving of two loaves of leavened bread from the wheat harvest. Since this holiday is 50 days from "Firstfruits," the Greek name for this holiday is Pentecost (from the prefix "pente," meaning five.) However, the Jewish people call it by the biblical name of "Shavuot."

Like the previous Feast of Firstfruits (see last chapter), this holiday also acknowledged God as the source of their agricultural blessings. Specifically, by giving to God some of the firstfruits of the land again. This time it was from the wheat harvest. As a matter of fact, the bountiful harvest (or lack thereof) was distinctly tied to Israel's commitment to the Mosaic Law. As the Mosaic law told them,

Deuteronomy 7:11-13

"Therefore you shall keep the commandment, the statutes, and the judgments which I command you today, to observe them. Then it shall come to pass, because you listen to these judgments, and keep and do them, that the LORD your God... will love you and bless you and multiply you; **He will also bless the fruit of your womb and the fruit of your land...**"

Just a side note here, while we should NEVER use the amount in our bank account as a barometer of the quality of our relationship with God (the book of Job teaches that as Job was a righteous man who lost everything), however we should take notice that if all of a sudden we experience a 'bump' or 'lack' in our financial life, perhaps God is trying to get our attention? Perhaps we have missed Him in something? Perhaps He is also trying to teach us something. The Mosaic Law distinctly taught that.

In ancient Israel, there were three times a year when all males were required to appear before the Lord. *"Three times in the year all your males shall appear before the Lord GOD."* (Exodus 23:17) Interestingly enough, all three were tied into the harvest and God's blessings. In the spring, it was Passover and the Feast of Firstfruits (the barley harvest). In the autumn, it was the Feast of Sukkot (Tabernacles) (the harvest of grapes and olives). Right here in the middle was the Feast of Weeks, associated with the wheat harvest.

Thus, all three "required attendance" holidays were tied into God's provisions. In other words, when God blesses, remember to thank Him.

In the Feast of Weeks, Israel was to take some of the finest flour from this wheat harvest and bake two loaves of bread and offer them up at the Temple (along with other items like lambs, bulls, goats, and rams.) Interestingly enough, these two loaves are baked with leaven. Leaven is usually associated with sin. Why is leaven accepted here? I'll answer that later.

Two loaves of bread were given
to the Lord on the 50th day

Remember at the beginning of this chapter, I said that
this holiday is not associated with any historical
event? Well, that may not be fully accurate.
According to the tradition of the rabbis, they have
deduced that since Israel left Egypt in the first month
(approximately April on our calendar), fifty days later
brings us to the third month (approximately June on
our calendar). And the scriptures tell us that
something historical did indeed happen during the
third month after Israel left Egypt.

<u>Exodus 19: 1&7</u>
*" In the third month after the children of Israel had
gone out of the land of Egypt, on the same day, they
came to the Wilderness of Sinai… So Moses came and
called for the elders of the people, and laid before
them **all these words** which the LORD commanded
him. "*

Therefore, since the Law (the 10 Commandments) was
given in this month, the rabbis felt confident enough

to associate this holiday with the giving of the Law. As Ruth Specter Lascelle says,

> *"The Jewish people call this day "Shavuot" or "Weeks" because it comes seven weeks after Passover. They are reminded on that day of 'The Ten Commandments' that were given to Moses fifty days after the Passover lamb was slain for their redemption from Egypt... This feast is also known by the name "Day of Giving of the Law."*

Now I don't always agree with rabbinical interpretations of the Law. However, regarding this one, the evidence (though circumstantial) seems good that the Law was actually given on the 50th day after Passover.

The rabbis tell us that "The Law" was given here on Mt. Sinai on the Feast of (seven) Weeks.

Notice that Exodus gives us some other unique details about that day. Do you remember what happened while Moses was up on the mountain receiving the Law? Aaron was down there making a golden calf for the people. And when he had finished it, they had a party worshipping this golden calf - as the God who delivered them from Egypt! And what happened when Moses came down?

<u>Exodus 32:15,19, 25-28</u>
And Moses turned and went down from the mountain, and the two tablets of the Testimony were in his hand... So it was, as soon as he came near the camp, that he saw the calf and the dancing. So Moses' anger

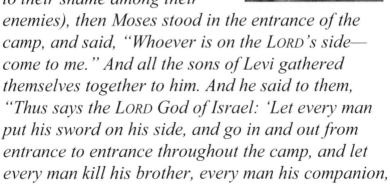

became hot, and he cast the tablets out of his hands and broke them at the foot of the mountain...

Now when Moses saw that the people were unrestrained (for Aaron had not restrained them, to their shame among their enemies), then Moses stood in the entrance of the camp, and said, "Whoever is on the LORD's side— come to me." And all the sons of Levi gathered themselves together to him. And he said to them, "Thus says the LORD God of Israel: 'Let every man put his sword on his side, and go in and out from entrance to entrance throughout the camp, and let every man kill his brother, every man his companion,

*and every man his neighbor.' " So the sons of Levi
did according to the word of Moses. And **about three
thousand men of the people fell that day.***

What a sad day! Three thousand Israelites died! They
broke the Law before it was ever given! But does that
specific number (3,000) ring a bell for you? Let's look
at the New Covenant Scriptures to see what happened
one 50th day after Firstfruits in Jerusalem during the
first century....

Acts 2:1-4

When the Day of Pentecost had fully come, they (the
disciples) *were all with one accord in one place. And
suddenly there came a sound from heaven, as of a
rushing mighty wind, and it filled the whole house
where they were sitting. Then there appeared to them
divided tongues, as of fire, and one sat upon each of
them. And they were all filled with the Holy Spirit and
began to speak with other tongues, as the Spirit gave
them utterance.*

*As a crowd gathers to see what is going on, Peter
preaches to the crowd. And then look what happens....*

Acts 2:40-41

*" And with many other words he testified and exhorted
them, saying, "Be saved from this perverse
generation." Then those who gladly received his word*

*were baptized; and that day about **three thousand souls** were added to them."*

There you have it! When the Law was given, 3,000 died. When the Holy Spirit was given, 3,000 were given life! Isn't that the case? The Law brings death (only because none of us can keep it), but Jesus brings life! The Law God gave is <u>good</u>, but it was given externally. Our sin nature causes us to break His good Law. But in Jesus, the Spirit of God gives us **a new heart** so that we can live a godly life and not break His Law! Isn't that what the Jewish prophets said would happen?

In the Temple courtyard – 3,000 people accepted the Messiah and gained new life

Jeremiah 31:31-33

"Behold, the days are coming, says the LORD, when I will make a new covenant with the house of Israel and with the house of Judah— not according to the covenant that I made with their fathers in the day that

I took them by the hand to lead them out of the land
of Egypt...But this is the covenant that I will make
with the house of Israel after those days, says the
*LORD: I will put My law in their minds, and **write it on***
their hearts...

And do you remember the **two** loaves of bread waved
on this day that I spoke about earlier in this chapter?
Well, on the 50th day after Jesus' death, Acts chapter
2 tells us of Peter's preaching on Pentecost to that big
crowd gathered in Jerusalem. And since it was
Jerusalem, it's safe to say that the majority of people in
the crowd were Jews. But there were certainly some
Gentiles in the crowd. They had come to believe in
and worship the God of Israel and become proselytes.
Therefore, since that day of Pentecost (when the
church was born), the congregation of believers is to
be made up of **two** distinct groups - saved Jews and
saved Gentiles! The two loaves are still waved
together as one! As Paul says, "*For He* [Messiah]
Himself is our peace, who has made both [Jew and
Gentile] *one, and has broken down the middle wall of*
separation;" (Ephesians 2:14)

And why were the loaves in Leviticus 23 baked and
offered to God with leaven? Because when we come
to God, it is as a sinner. We all (Jew and Gentile) still
have a sin nature that will not fully be removed until
we reach glory. God knows that. He understands. We
are accepted and saved with our sin nature still there.
Now, that does **not** give us an excuse for sin, not at

all. But when you fight against that old sin nature, which wants to do evil, know that God understands. Remember that He has given us the victory over sin through the Holy Spirit, whom He gave to all believers, beginning on the Jewish Feast of Weeks.

Endnotes

6) Ruth Specter Lascelle, Jewish Faith and the New Covenant (Fairfield, Ohio: Rock of Israel, 1993), hardcover edition p. 269.

The Summer Interval

*When you reap the harvest of your land, you shall not
wholly reap the corners of your field when you reap,
nor shall you gather any gleaning from your harvest.
You shall leave them for the poor and for the
stranger: I am the LORD your God.*

Leviticus chapter 23: verse 22

Once the Feast of Weeks is over, we then embark
upon a time when there are no holidays in Israel for a
significant amount of time. For basically the whole
summer season, many Israelites went back to their
homes and did what they were meant to do: work in
the fields. *"When you reap the harvest of your land..."*
(Leviticus 23:22a). So we see that there are times to
worship God and other times that we are expected to
work.

And if you notice, God tells them that in the midst of
their work to not forget those who are less fortunate
than they are. God tells them to remember "the poor
and the stranger." Throughout scripture, we see that
God always has a special place in His heart for the
poor and alien. Israel was instructed to never take
advantage of the poor or the alien. One reason is
because Israel was a stranger in Egypt themselves. So

56

they should know what it feels like to be a stranger in a strange land. As a matter of fact, in helping the poor, God considered it as a personal loan that He Himself will repay!

He who has pity on the poor lends to the LORD,
And He will pay back what he has given.

Let me ask you a question. How do we, as believers, help the poor? While it is currently true that in America most people generally don't have impoverished people dwelling next door to us. Yet, how many Christians go out to eat on a Sunday afternoon, after church, and make a big show of praying at the table. Then they demand perfect service from their waitress and finally go home, leaving the table with tons of empty plates and a very small tip for her or even no tip at all and just a gospel tract! That, my friends, is an insult to God.

Do you think that waitress enjoys giving up her Sunday mornings with her family to wait on you? Isn't she probably working to help feed her children at home? Wouldn't God look at her as 'poor' and be concerned with her welfare? Be generous to those who need it. In helping the poor, God remembers your deeds.

At that time, Israel had no politicians. No social welfare programs in place. Therefore, in letting the poor and stranger go through the fields to glean what was left, that was the primary method many poor people used to feed their families. They depended upon people's willingness to not be greedy and strip their fields bare. They depended upon people's willingness to obey God and remember the poor and stranger in the land.

In looking at the bigger picture with the first four feasts in view, we see that the last feast in history to be fulfilled prophetically was the Feast of Weeks (Pentecost). That was fulfilled in Acts chapter 2 and discussed in the last chapter. The next one to be fulfilled prophetically is the Feast of Trumpets and is discussed in the following chapter. Thus, believers need to realize that we are prophetically living in a period of time in between Feast four (Pentecost) and Feast five (Trumpets).

SPRING	SUMMER	AUTUMN
Feasts 1,2,3,4	(We are here)	Feasts 5,6,7

Did you ever go to the State Park and look at those big maps of the different hiking trails available? Don't you look at that large map and search for that big red dot somewhere on it? And it usually has those three special words next to it, "*You are here*." Well, if you write in the margins of your Bible, you need to write next to verse 22 in big letters, "We Are Here."

So what did Israel do during this time in between Feasts four and five? Verse 22 tells them to work in the fields. Reap the harvest, remember people. Since the body of Messiah was born on Pentecost (Feast number four) almost 2,000 years ago, what are we supposed to be doing now? Work in the fields. Reaping the harvest. Remembering people. Is the harvest today agriculture? No, it's people. Look what Jesus said...

John 4:35
Do you not say, 'There are still four months and then comes the harvest'? Behold, I say to you, lift up your eyes and look at the fields, for they are already white for harvest!

The problem is not with the harvest, but with lack of workers!

Luke 10:2
Then He said to them, "The harvest truly is great, but the laborers are few; therefore pray the Lord of the harvest to send out laborers into His harvest.

And what is the message of the harvest? How do we reap a soul? Tell them about repentance and the good news about heaven. And what is the good news? Well, first let me tell you what most unbelievers think the way to heaven is. The average answer on the street to the question, "How would you get to heaven?" probably would be, "Well, I've tried to live a good life." Buzz! Wrong answer! (Want to try a lifeline, Regis?) Trusting in living a 'good life' is **not** the gospel. As a matter of fact, it's the **opposite** of the gospel.

The Bible (and our own hearts) tells us that we have not lived a perfect life. No one (except Jesus) has lived a perfect life. *"But we are all like an unclean thing, And all our righteousnesses are like filthy rags;"* (Isaiah 64:6) *"As it is written, There is none righteous, no, not one"* (Romans 3:10) Good and righteous works are fine. But they are not going to get anyone to heaven. Why? Because sins keep people out of heaven. And for unbelievers, sins pollute even the good they may have done in life.

So what is the gospel? To put it simply in a word, it is a <u>switch</u>. Jesus died for our sins, and we receive His righteousness as a free gift. He took our bad; we get His good credited to us. That's it! You have to be as perfect as God to get into heaven. We can't be that good (in our natural selves), but we can receive the goodness of God as a free gift by faith. *"For by grace you have been saved through faith, and that not of yourselves; it is the gift of God..."* (Ephesians 2:8)

And who needs this gift? The poor and the stranger. Well, first we are to remember that this means the physically poor and stranger. But additionally, who else is poor? The person who doesn't know the Lord. He really is poor! (And I don't care how rich Elon

Musk is, if he doesn't know the Lord, he really is a poor, poor man.) And who is the stranger? Those who don't know our God. They are strangers. "

Ephesians 2:12

[Remember] that at that time you were without [Messiah], being aliens from the commonwealth of Israel and strangers from the covenants of promise, having no hope and without God in the world.

God told Israel to <u>remember people</u> during harvest time. The time of harvest is now. Are you and I remembering people?

The Feast of Trumpets

Speak to the children of Israel, saying: 'In the seventh month, on the first day of the month, you shall have a sabbath-rest, a memorial of blowing of trumpets, a holy convocation.

Leviticus chapter 23: verse 24

The long summer has finished. After the summer silence, the next holiday occurs, and it's a loud one. The Jewish people call this day **Rosh Hashanah** (lit: Head of the Year), but according to the Law, it is specifically called **Yom Turah** ("Day of Shouting"), and it always occurs on the first day of the seventh month. The month is called Tishri, and it always occurs in the autumn season, usually in mid to late September.

For this holiday, many Jewish people send each other New Year's cards and wish each other a "Happy New Year", but this is merely a Rabbinic interpretation of this holiday. Nowhere in the Law is the first day of this seventh month called Rosh Hashanah.

Sample of a Rosh HaShana greeting
card sent today.

One of the reasons ancient rabbis looked to this day
as the beginning of the New Year is that if you
rearrange the Hebrew letters of Genesis 1:1, "In the
beginning," you actually get Aleph b' Tishri (the 1st
day of Tishri). So the rabbis deduced that the
creation of the world occurred on this day. That's a
unique way of looking at it, but I wouldn't put any
faith in it.

These days are supposed to be a very somber time
of year for the Jewish people. The rabbis have
taught that the ten days between Rosh Hashanah
and Yom Kippur (the next holy day on the calendar)
are known as the ten "Days of Awe." They teach
that during these days, the fate of your future hangs
in the balance with God. On this day, they claim,
God begins to review the records. He looks at His

heavenly books. He looks at the sins of His people and, according to what His records show, decides each person's fate for the upcoming year. That's why such great importance is placed upon the act of repentance (T'shuvah) during these days.

According to the traditional Jewish view, there are three books in heaven. The book containing the names of the righteous, the book containing the names of the wicked, and the book containing the names of those in the middle, so to speak.

The Bible clearly speaks of
record books in heaven.

The names of the righteous are inscribed for a good year, the names of the wicked are inscribed for a bad year (including possible death), and those in the middle are given these ten days to change their ways (T'shuvah /repent) because they will no longer have time after Yom Kippur, merely ten days away. On that day the books are sealed. Your fate is unchangeable. That is why, if you look at many Jewish New Year cards, they contain the phrase

"L'shanah tovah tikkaevu - May you be inscribed for a good year."

While I personally don't believe the rabbinic tradition concerning these dates as the basis for a good or bad year (since the book of Job shows us that some 'good' people do have bad years), I do believe that there are books kept in heaven that God reviews. The reason I believe this is because the Bible teaches this and not tradition.

Malachi 3:16

*Then those who feared the LORD spoke to one another, And the LORD listened and heard them; So **a book of remembrance** was **written** before Him. For those who fear the LORD And who meditate on His name.*

Revelation 20:12

*And I saw the dead, small and great, standing before God, **and books were opened**. And **another book** was opened, which is **the Book of Life**.*

Exodus 32:33

*And the LORD said to Moses, "Whoever has sinned against Me, I will blot him out of **My book**.*

Philippians 4:3

And I urge you also, true companion, help these women who labored with me in the gospel, with

*Clement also, and the rest of my fellow workers, whose names are in **the Book of Life**.*

Luke 10:20

*Nevertheless do not rejoice in this, that the spirits are subject to you, but rather rejoice because your names are **written** in heaven."*

So from these scriptures, we can see that God does indeed have at least one book called the Book of Life in heaven. Some people believe that all people are born with their names already inscribed in the book of life (and therefore all babies who die go to heaven), but when you reach an age of accountability (and there is no consensus on when that age is) and when you sin willfully, your name is taken out of that book. It's only when you are born again that your name is then restored to the Book of Life.

Believers in Jesus can rejoice that our names are promised to be there when we arrive. It's not 'feeling' saved or 'trying' to be saved that gets our name there, but it is faith in Messiah. Trusting in Jesus to place our names there. He has promised, "All that the Father gives Me will come to Me, and the one who comes to Me I will by no means cast out." (John 6:37)

Growing up in New York City, I still remember being in synagogue during this holiday. From our apartment, we would walk about 4 or 5 blocks to the "Shul" (a Yiddish nickname for the synagogue) and then spend 2 or 3 hours at the service. The service was basically one that went on all day long with people coming and going during the service as they pleased. Many times my family would go to Shul for an hour or two in the morning and then go home and have lunch. In the evening, we would come back for the remainder of the service - with many of the same people still there! The service was almost all in Hebrew, so often times, as a young boy, I would wander around the back rooms of the old synagogue to keep my interest up.

As an interesting side note, part of this holiday involved the whole congregation going on a field trip. Really, it did. At some point during this holiday, the whole congregation would go out into the narthex of the synagogue and fill our pockets (or a brown paper bag) with lots of breadcrumbs. Then we would walk about 3 blocks down to the Bronx River. (It really was more like a creek than a river, but hey, it was a field trip.) After a few prayers, we would cast all our crumbs into the river and watch them float away. This Jewish tradition is based upon a verse from the Jewish prophet Micah. "You will cast all our sin into the depths of the sea." (Micah 7:19b) As you can see, Jewish tradition is very big with 'hands on' lessons. I have no problem with that.

Back to the synagogue now. I still remember a distinct part of the Rosh Hashanah service that I always enjoyed. It was hearing the sound of the shofar. The sound of the shofar would powerfully resonate through that long sanctuary, and it always got my attention.

The sound of the Shofar is heard around the world on the Feast of Trumpets.

While the materials used for the shofar can vary around the world, it's typically a ram's horn that is blown. However, it can also be from an antelope, gazelle, or any other Levitically clean (kosher) animal. Incidentally, they will never use a cow's horn in the synagogue. The reason? It's due to that little incident when we came out of Egypt. You remember that golden calf incident? When Aaron threw the people's gold into the fire and out popped the golden calf! Then Israel bowed down to worship it. Well, that cow brings back some bad memories for us, and we don't want to remind God of our bad past now, do we? So that's why they prefer a ram's horn.

Actually, the sounding of the ram's horn is supposed to bring back some **good** memories for the Jewish people. It's an event called "The Akedah" and is from Genesis 22. Let's look at that event. At the request of God, Abraham had willingly laid his only son, Isaac, on the wooden altar he had just built upon Mount Moriah. He was about to plunge the knife into Isaac when an angel of the Lord stopped him. It turns out it was only a test.

<u>Genesis 22:10-13</u>
And Abraham stretched out his hand and took the knife to slay his son. But the Angel of the LORD called to him from heaven and said, "Abraham, Abraham!" So he said, "Here I am." And He said, "Do not lay your hand on the lad, or do anything to

him; for now I know that you fear God, since you have not withheld your son, your only son, from Me." Then Abraham lifted his eyes and looked, and there behind him was a ram caught in a thicket by its horns. So Abraham went and took the ram, and offered it up for a burnt offering instead of his son.

This event is one that Judaism looks up to very much. This text is read by many in synagogue during Rosh Hashanah, and some religious Jewish people even look to the righteousness of Abraham as merit for themselves before God. How good it is to know that just as Abraham did not hold back his only unique son, Isaac, from sacrifice, God did not hold back His only unique Son, Messiah Jesus, from sacrifice.

Isaac went willingly to his 'death' and lay upon that altar of wood without protest. So did Jesus. However, here's where the similarity breaks down. A ram was ultimately sacrificed as a substitute for Isaac. Jesus did not take a substitute for His own life, but rather He became the substitute for you and me! That's good news, isn't it? To have someone die in your place. That's why they call it the "gospel" (good news).

But most importantly for this chapter, let me talk about the Feast of Trumpets and its significance for believers today. The real focus of this day for us is the sounding of the shofar. After all, it's called the Feast of Trumpets! As believers, those of us who know the Bible are indeed waiting for a shofar to sound one day. A very loud one. The real trumpet blast we should be waiting for is going to sound from heaven! As Rabbi Paul says...

1 Corinthians 15:51-52

Behold, I tell you a mystery: We shall not all sleep, but we shall all be changed— in a moment, in the twinkling of an eye, at the last <u>trumpet</u>. For the <u>trumpet</u> will sound, and the dead will be raised incorruptible, and we shall be changed.

1 Thessalonians 4:16-18

For the Lord Himself will descend from heaven with a shout, with the voice of an archangel, and with the <u>trumpet</u> of God. And the dead in [Messiah] will rise first. Then we who are alive and remain shall be caught up together with them in the clouds to meet the Lord in the air. And thus we shall always be with the Lord. Therefore comfort one another with these words.

That worldwide shofar blast will indicate the Lord's return for us. The popular name of this event is called "The Rapture," and we have every reason to believe that it could be in our lifetime. At that moment, believers from all over the globe will meet the Lord in the air. Billions of other people will be left behind to rapidly undergo a series of events found in the book of Revelation.

Don't think God can 'rapture' people like that? He already has! In the Old Testament it has happened not once, but twice before! Think of Elijah going up to heaven in a whirlwind. (See 2 Kings 2:11.)

Also consider the fact that Enoch walked with God and was no more, because God took him (i.e., raptured him). (See Genesis 5:24 and Hebrews 11:5). So let's not forget that our real hope in this life, as believers, is not waiting for the "Under-taker" to come for us, but it's waiting for the "Upper-taker" to come for us!

John 14:3

And if I go and prepare a place for you, I will come again and receive you to Myself; that where I am, *there* you may be also.

Amen! Come, Messiah Jesus. We're waiting for You.

The Day of Atonement

Also the tenth day of this seventh month shall be the Day of Atonement. It shall be a holy convocation for you; you shall afflict your souls, and offer an offering made by fire to the LORD.

Leviticus chapter 23: verse 27

A mere ten days after the Feast of Trumpets comes one of the holiest and most solemn days on the Jewish calendar. Yom Kippur (literally, Day of Covering) is a national day of repentance and forgiveness. The culmination of the "Ten Days of Awe" (which began on the Feast of Trumpets) now ends with Yom Kippur. If a person hasn't repented by Yom Kippur, the rabbis can't offer a person much hope after that.

On the eve of Yom Kippur, Jewish people around the world gather in their synagogues and will refuse all food, all pleasure, and all work for the next 24 hours. A total fast is extrapolated from Leviticus for a Jewish person to "*afflict his soul*" (Lev. 16:29), and traditionally this means no food or water.

As Ruth Specter Lascelle explains:

"God commanded the Jewish people to keep a day of atonement, a day in which they shall

mourn for their sins (afflict their souls), a day of covering, of forgiveness, in which they are to cease from their own labor and bring a sacrifice offering to God."

There are really several components to this day. On an individual level, fasting was required for the people to afflict their souls. But in Jerusalem during the Temple times, individuals had a single representative before God on Yom Kippur. It was the High Priest. His complete service to God is outlined in Leviticus 16, but just part of his day is listed below:

*Washing himself and changing his clothes to clean linen garments.

*Making atonement for himself and his family with a bull.

*Taking a goat and sacrificing it as a sin offering for Israel.

*Taking a second goat, the scapegoat, and confessing Israel's sins onto it.

*Having someone lead that goat into the wilderness - never to be seen again.

*Carrying a portable incense maker to make lots of smoky incense so that his vision was clouded as he entered into the room called the "Holy of Holies."

*Entering behind the veil into the Holy of Holies and sprinkling the bulls' and the goats' blood onto the mercy seat and in front of it seven times.

The High Priest alone was allowed to enter into the Holy of Holies - only once a year.

When the day was over and everything had been done correctly, then it could be said atonement was made for the year.

<u>Leviticus 16:30</u>
For on that day the priest shall make atonement for you, to cleanse you, that you may be clean from all your sins before the LORD.

You see, according to the Law, it was always **blood** that made atonement.

Leviticus 17:11

*'For the life of the flesh is in the blood, and I have
given it to you upon the altar to make atonement for
your souls; for it is the blood that makes atonement
for the soul.'*

This 'blood makes atonement' principle is not a New
Testament, concept as some Jewish people would like
to have us believe, but one set down by God Himself
through Moses centuries before the New Testament
was ever written. The New Covenant writer says the
same thing: *"...and without shedding of blood there is
no remission."* (Hebrews 9:22)

Today, of course, if you went to Jerusalem on the Day
of Atonement and wanted to see this whole ceremony
with the High Priest going into the Holy of Holies,
carrying in the blood to sprinkle, you would be
waiting a long time. None of this happens anymore.
The reason? The Roman army destroyed the Temple
in the year 70 A.D.

Since that time, no sacrifices have been offered by
Israel on the Day of Atonement. Jesus Himself
predicted that one day the Temple itself would be
destroyed. That statement must have taken the
disciples by surprise....

Matthew 24:1-2

*Then Jesus went out and departed from the temple,
and His disciples came up to show Him the buildings*

of the temple. And Jesus said to them, "Do you not see all these things? Assuredly, I say to you, not one stone shall be left here upon another, that shall not be thrown down."

Jesus made that prediction around 30 A.D. It took just 40 years to fulfill. Today, the destruction of Jerusalem is written about in every modern encyclopedia. Historians of that time period, like Josephus, tell us of that terrible day. In addition to the Temple being destroyed in 70 A.D., it is estimated that 1.3 million Jewish people lost their lives at the hands of the Roman soldiers around that same time. The Romans were squelching a revolt. They were not playing games. It was a devastating year for Israel.

Only a retaining 'wall' remains of a Temple area once destroyed by the Romans. As a result, no blood sacrifices are done anymore by Israel.

Since that time, no sacrifices have been offered in Jerusalem by Israel. The Temple has never been rebuilt. Therefore, the focus of the Day of Atonement has shifted from a day focused upon the High Priest making atonement for Israel (through blood) to a day of individual fasting for forgiveness.

In synagogues today, a focal point of the Yom Kippur service is called the "Kol Nidre" service. It literally means "All Vows." Part of forgiveness, the rabbis teach, is asking God to forgive any false vows they have made during the past year. It is well known to any student of Jewish history that during the 'dark ages' of Europe, many Jews were required to take a vow of Christian faith and forced to submit to baptism at the hands of "Church" leaders in exchange for their lives. (The "Church" leaders falsely thought this oath and baptism would save Jewish souls and considered this a worthy thing to do.) In fear of their lives, many Jews took the oath and submitted to forced baptism. It was during Yom Kippur that they asked God to forgive them for what they felt was accepting allegiance to a false religion. Thus, the "Kol Nidre," or the absolution of vows service, was born.

Also, eight times during the Yom Kippur service are the Al-Het (The Confessions) prayers made. As Ruth Specter Lascelle explains...

"At this part of the prayers, all the worshippers beat their chests and admit that they are guilty for many sins which are listed and which they read. Though each individual has not committed every specific sins, all as a united group are considered guilty for those of others, and therefore the prayer is in the plural and includes the nation of Israel. Confession is the main theme of the Yom Kippur service, for the Jewish religion teaches that if a man sincerely repents or regrets his misdeeds, he will be forgiven. The Al-Het enumerates many kinds of sins such as dishonesty, cruelty, gluttony, treachery, disrespect for parents, stubbornness, haughtiness, hardening of the heart, foolish speech, tale bearing, etc." 2

So by looking at what this day represents, I think you can see the seriousness of it all. I remember as a child coming home from synagogue and not being able to turn on a light switch because that was considered work. Before we would leave for synagogue that evening, we would determine which lights would stay on and which lights would stay off for the next 24 hours. How frightened I was when, as a child, by force of habit, I returned home and turned on a light switch one evening.

Some points to remember about Yom Kippur:

- It was a day focused upon the High Priest making a blood sacrifice
- It was National Day of Repentance

- It was a day for no human work
- The modern day focus is one of fasting and repentance without a blood sacrifice

Reading the scriptures today, I see the place that Yom Kippur plays in the big picture of God's prophetic calendar. "Work" in scripture is always symbolic of man's efforts. However, before a holy God, our "work" always will fall short. Isaiah 64:6 says, *"And all our righteousnesses are like filthy rags;"* In other words, no good works will make us completely righteous before God. Good works are indeed good, but they cannot save anyone from their sins. A thief, before a judge on Friday, cannot proclaim his good works of Monday through Thursday and then expect to get off on that basis. And a sinner cannot expect to proclaim their goodness before God and expect that to be the basis for His forgiveness. Good works are good when they are done and God always approves of us doing good, however they don't procure forgiveness for sins.

As a believer now, I can see that the 'no work' God commanded Israel on this day points forward to the real day when Israel will do 'no work' for their salvation. Why? Because they will (one day in the future) realize that Jesus, their Messiah, did all the work for them - to bring them complete atonement. They just have to 'accept' His free gift, not earn it or work for it. Just look at these verses that tell the same story....

Zechariah 12:10

And I will pour on the house of David and on the inhabitants of Jerusalem the Spirit of grace and supplication; **then they will look on Me whom they pierced.** *Yes, they will mourn for Him as one mourns for his only son, and grieve for Him as one grieves for a firstborn.*

.

Zechariah 13:1

In that day *a fountain shall be opened for the house of David and for the inhabitants of Jerusalem, for sin and for uncleanness.*

Matthew 23:39

...for I say to you [Jerusalem], you shall see Me [Jesus] no more till you say, 'Blessed is He who comes in the name of the LORD!'

When will this happen? When do people usually cry out to receive the Lord in their life? When things go good - or when things go bad? When things go bad, right? So too, it will be with Israel. Israel will accept their Messiah <u>after</u> the worst time in history. After the trumpet sounds (after the Rapture), Israel will begin to go through **the** specific time period in history called "The Great Tribulation" (see the book of Revelation for more details.) This time is also called the time of "Jacob's trouble." It is when the Anti-Messiah will rule the world, and his hatred of the Jews will be fierce.

<u>Jeremiah 30:7</u>
Alas! For that day is great, So that none is like it; And it is the time of <u>Jacob's trouble</u>, But he shall be saved out of it.

<u>Daniel 12:1</u>
At that time Michael shall stand up, The great prince who stands watch over the sons of your people; And there shall <u>be a time of trouble</u>, Such as never was since there was a nation, Even to that time.

<u>Daniel 12:7</u>
...when the power of the holy people (Israel) *has been <u>completely shattered</u>, all these things shall be finished.*

You can study the book of Revelation and Matthew chapter 24 for even more details of this time period. But, at the end of those terrible days (which are still to come), Israel will be at their wit's end. As Daniel says, their power will be 'completely shattered.' Then they will truly realize that 'no works' will save them.

They will realize that Jesus was/is their blood sacrifice. That He is their High Priest. That He is their atonement. And as Rabbi Paul says in Romans 11:26, "And so all Israel will be saved."

While other believers will have honest views on the end times (and that is fine), I believe Israel's national atonement will take place after the Rapture occurs. It all seems to fit prophetically.

Endnotes

1) Ruth Specter Lascelle, Jewish Faith and the New Covenant, p. 294
2) Ibid, p. 301

84

The Feast of Tabernacles

Speak to the children of Israel, saying: 'The fifteenth day of this seventh month shall be the Feast of Tabernacles for seven days to the LORD And you shall take for yourselves on the first day the fruit of beautiful trees, branches of palm trees, the boughs of leafy trees, and willows of the brook; and you shall rejoice before the LORD your God for seven days.

Leviticus chapter 23: verses 34&40

Sins have just been forgiven on the Day of Atonement, so what atmosphere do you think the next feast will adopt? A sad or happy one? A happy one, of course! Aren't those newly forgiven the happiest? So, just five days after Yom Kippur comes the celebration called the Feast of Tabernacles (also called the Feast of Booths). This holiday is rich with joy and symbolism.

The focus of the holiday is the building of temporary booths or shelters. The time of the festival fell in the autumn, when the end harvest of the main fruits of the ground, the corn, the grapes, the wine, and the oil, were all gathered in. Dr. Joseph Fuiten points out how many Jewish families celebrate Tabernacles today:

"At home, each family builds a booth in their yard (or on a balcony if necessary) and decorates it with palm and other leafy branches. It is then trimmed with fruits and vegetables and homemade decorations. Each day the family spends time in it (usually a meal). The booth is not to be made solid like a tree house, but one should be able to look up and see a few stars. It is to commemorate God's sheltering presence in a fragile existence." 1

For seven days, Israel lives in temporary shelters called "Tabernacles"

Actually, the first 'tabernacles' we see in scripture is when Israel came out of Egypt and dwelt in tabernacles (or booths) for forty years in the wilderness.

<u>Numbers 24: 2,3,5</u>
And Balaam raised his eyes, and saw Israel encamped according to their tribes; and the Spirit of God came

upon him. Then he took up his oracle and said...
How lovely are your tents, O Jacob! Your dwellings,
O Israel!"

Though Israel dwelt in tents or tabernacles for forty
years, they were completely taken care of. God
Himself provided for all their needs. Moses reminded
them of this publicly: *"These forty years the LORD*
your God has been with you; you have lacked
nothing." (Deuteronomy 2:7) It seems fitting that
God would want to remind Israel of how He provided
for them in the past. So why not trust Him for their
future? Isn't that something that we all need to hear
from time to time?

During Jesus' time, there were some significant
features about this holiday that occurred at the
Temple. One of them was the 'pouring out of water'
ceremony. Since this feast is at the beginning of the
rainy season in Israel, the pouring out of water at the
Temple symbolically asks God to send them the rain
that they, an agricultural society, so desperately need
for their future crops to grow. Today, we often take
the abundance of water in our country for granted.
They didn't.

Just as the Ark was brought into Jerusalem as a great event, so did the water drawing ceremony each year produce great celebration.

Part of this ceremony involved the high priest taking an empty golden pitcher and walking to the pool of Siloam. There he was to fill it with water from the pool and make his way back to the Temple where that water was poured into a basin at the foot of the altar. Of course there was great pomp and ceremony while all this was going on.

Although physical water was used, the water was also symbolic of something more. It was symbolic of their desire for God to pour out His Spirit upon them. As Dr. Fuiten writes:

> According to Edersheim, in his book 'The Temple', the Talmud teaches that this day is called "the drawing out of water' because it refers to Isaiah 12:3 and the drawing out from the wells of salvation. The rain represented the Holy Spirit and the water drawing pointed to

the day when God would rain his Spirit on all
Israel.

Knowing all this now, doesn't it make Jesus'
statement during the Feast of Tabernacles that much
more appropriate?

John 7:37-38

On the last day, that great day of the feast
(Tabernacles)*, Jesus stood and cried out, saying, "If
anyone thirsts, let him come to Me and drink. He who
believes in Me, as the Scripture has said, out of his
heart will flow rivers of living water."*

Israel had just seen the High Priest pouring out water.
He was asking for rain and, symbolically speaking,
asking for the Spirit of God. Then Jesus stands up in
Jerusalem and makes this announcement - that if
anyone is thirsty, they should come to Him for a drink.
It makes sense now, doesn't it? Interestingly enough,
when Jesus heals a man born blind, where does He
send him to wash? The pool of Siloam, where this
water had just been drawn from! (See John 9:7)
Maybe Jesus was trying to show all those in Jerusalem
that their prayers for the Spirit could only be fulfilled
in Him.

The Feast of Tabernacles also has several interesting
minor components to it as well. First is the number
seven. Seven is the number of completion in the
Bible. If you look at all the sacrifices for the Feast of

Tabernacles in Numbers chapter 29, you'll see some very interesting numerical patterns:

- The Feast of Tabernacles had 7 days to it
- It was in the 7th month of the year
- It was the 7th Feast of the year
- There were 70 bulls sacrificed during the Feast
- There were 14 rams sacrificed during the Feast
- There were 7 goats sacrificed during the Feast
- There were 98 lambs sacrificed during the Feast

All those numbers are multiples of 7, the number symbolizing completion or perfection. The hallmark number of perfection and completion is stamped all over this feast!

The other interesting component to Tabernacles is that this feast had a 'Gentile' stamp on it. If you open up to Genesis chapter 10 and count the number of Gentile nations that formed after the worldwide flood, the number you get is seventy. 70 bulls sacrificed during Tabernacles and 70 nations listed in Genesis 10. This reminds me that Israel, as a priestly nation, was supposed to intercede for the Gentile nations.

And now to a major point that I believe the Bible clearly teaches about the Feast of Tabernacles and its relationship to the Gentiles. It's the final harvest. The final year-end harvest of Israel during Tabernacles points to the final harvest in the conversion of the

Gentile world. Why do I believe this? Because the prophet Zechariah clearly tells us that this feast is associated with Gentiles.

When the Feast of Trumpets (the Rapture) has been fulfilled. And when Israel has finally accepted Jesus' atonement. When Feasts 5 & 6 have been fulfilled prophetically. When she has finally said to Jesus, *"Blessed is He who comes in the Name of the Lord."* (Matthew 23:39) When the culmination of the book of Revelation is at its peak. When all the Gentile nations have gathered together against Jerusalem to battle. Then all the things in Zechariah 14 will finally come to pass.

Zechariah 14: 1-4
For I will gather all the nations to battle against Jerusalem; The city shall be taken, The houses rifled, and the women ravished. Half of the city shall go into captivity, but the remnant of the people shall not be cut off from the city. Then the LORD will go forth and fight against those nations, as He fights in the day of battle. And in that day His feet will stand on the Mount of Olives, Which faces Jerusalem on the east. And the Mount of Olives shall be split in two,

Whose feet are those on the Mt. of Olives? The Messiah, Jesus!

This photo was taken from the Mount of Olives looking towards Jerusalem. Jesus will return to this mountain.

<u>Zechariah 14: 5b</u>
Thus the LORD my God will come, and all the saints <u>with</u> You.

Notice, verse 5 says that Jesus comes **with** the saints (that's us believers). At the trumpet blast (the rapture), we meet Him in the air, but at His return, we come with Him to earth. And He does **not** take us to Rome, nor does He take us to Paris, or to the United Nations building. No, He takes us to Jerusalem. Why? To take up David's throne. To fulfill the answer to the disciples question in Acts 1:6, *" Lord, will You at this time restore the kingdom to Israel?"* Yes, then it will finally be the time! It will be time to set up His Kingdom on earth.

Zechariah 14:9

And the L*ORD* *shall be King over all the earth.*
In that day it shall be— "The L*ORD* *is one," And*
His name one.

There will be only **one** named followed on this planet.
That's it for all the other names followed - names like
Buddha, Krishna, or similar. From that moment on,
there will be only **one** name acknowledged, Yeshua
(Jesus' Hebrew name), as King of Kings and Lord of
Lords! And every knee will bow, and every tongue
will confess that Jesus is Lord! *"That at the name of*
Jesus every knee should bow" (Philippians 2:10).

When Jesus returns to this earth, there will be no more
war, no more starvation, no more corruption, just as
Isaiah foresaw:

Isaiah 2:2-4

Now it shall come to pass in the latter days that the
mountain of the L*ORD's* *house shall be established on*
the top of the mountains, and shall be exalted above
the hills; ***And all nations shall flow to it****. Many*
people shall come and say, "Come, and let us go up to
the mountain of the L*ORD, to the house of the God of*
Jacob; He will teach us His ways, and we shall walk
in His paths."

For out of Zion shall go forth the law, and the word of
the L*ORD from Jerusalem.* ***He*** *shall judge between the*

nations, and rebuke many people; they shall beat their swords into plowshares, and their spears into pruning hooks; Nation shall not lift up sword against nation, neither shall they learn war anymore.

One day, the nations will all stream into Jerusalem and have a righteous King to come to, Jesus, the Jewish Messiah. This is just as Zachariah foresaw in the Feats of Tabernacles.

Zechariah 14:16
*And it shall come to pass that everyone who is left of all the nations which came against Jerusalem shall go up from year to year to worship the King, the LORD of hosts, **__and to keep the Feast of Tabernacles__**.*

Sounds like a wonderful time to me. Who would not want to be a part of this? It's called the Kingdom of God. And Israel's joy and abundance at this last feast, the Feast of Tabernacles, is just a simple foreshadowing of it all. The best is yet to come.

1 Corinthians 2:9
Eye has not seen, nor ear heard, nor have entered into the heart of man the things which God has prepared for those who love Him.

Endnotes

1) Dr. Joseph B. Fuiten, Special Appointments with God (Bothell, Washington: Self-Published, 2000), p.78.
2) Ibid., p. 79

<u>*Summary*</u>

Now the Lord had said to Abram:
"Get out of your country,
From your family
And from your father's house,
To a land that I will show you.
I will make you a great nation;
I will bless you
And make your name great;
And you shall be a blessing.
I will bless those who bless you,
And I will curse him who curses you;
And in you all the families of the earth shall be
blessed.
Genesis 12:1-3

I believe that since the call of Abraham, God has had a
plan for Israel and that plan includes you and me.
Israel has a glorious future awaiting her. (And so do
all believers in Jesus as well.) Mind you, this is not
because of anything in Israel, but solely because of
God's grace. *"For the gifts and the calling of God are*
irrevocable." (Romans 11:29)

Abraham was called of God many centuries ago, and
Israel was called of God many centuries ago. They
were called to be a light to the nations. (See Isaiah
49:6) God does not change. That calling was never

taken away. Israel is still God's chosen people, although they are not walking in the fullness of God's blessings at the present time. However, God began the calendar with Israel's redemption from Egypt and ends it with Israel's rejoicing in abundance. Let us never forget that the best is yet to come.

But I would be remiss if I didn't make a personal application for each one reading this. You can't skip the order that God has ordained. He began the calendar with blood on the doorposts for Israel. He ended it with Israel rejoicing.

First things first. How are you planning to approach God on that day? What is on the doorpost of your own heart? If there is anything less than the blood of the spotless lamb, Yeshua / Jesus, on it, then I can certainly tell you, according to the word of God, that you are not prepared to meet God. While in Egypt, if Israel had put anything less than the blood of that spotless lamb on their doorposts, their firstborn would have been dead that evening. The spotless lamb saved them from death. Nothing more, nothing less.

Today, we have the choice to place on our hearts what we will. Do we place our own good deeds on the doorposts of our hearts, or do we trust in Jesus' precious atoning blood? The choice is ours. There is no other way to begin God's calendar. The ending is glorious. I pray that the words of the famous hymn are yours as they are mine. "My hope is built on nothing less than Jesus' blood and righteousness."

Jesus in the Seven Feasts of Israel

The Feast	He fulfills it!
Passover	He is the Lamb
Unleavened Bread	He removes our leaven (sin)
Firstfruits	He rose from the dead first
Seven Weeks	He gave the Spirit
Trumpets	He will return with a trumpet blast
Atonement	Israel will one day have atonement
Tabernacles	The whole world will rejoice

Doug Carmel's testimony

I was born in the 1960s to a newly immigrated Israeli man and a first-generation American born Jewish woman. Their marriage lasted only one short year. Eventually, my mother left and went back to her mother's house. It was under the care of these two Jewish women that I received much of my traditional Jewish upbringing.

My mother had to find work to support us, which meant that much of my time was spent with a dear Jewish immigrant from the old country affectionately known as my grandmother. She spoke fluent Yiddish, and as a result I learned to understand much of the old country language.

My grandmother's sense of traditionalism burned bright against the gentile background I'd grown accustomed to in earlier years. We kept two sets of silverware: one for milk and one for meat. We lit annual Yortzit candles in memory of her husband, my grandfather. We also observed special days, the Jewish holidays in the spring and fall. We were a very typical Jewish home in New York City!

While most of my friends were allowed to play ball on the street almost every October day, however, there were two specific days during that month that I was not to participate. It was not under the threat of violence that I abstained, but rather from a sense of belonging to my people. On the holy days of Yom Kippur and Rosh HaShanna we simply did not act as the gentiles did. I was told that Yom Kippur was the day that we were to fast so God would forgive us of our sins. We were not to engage in any normal activities that day - not even turning on a light switch. You can imagine how difficult this must have been for this ten year old, but we were Jewish! And if this is what God wanted us to do...

As I entered my teens, however, I began to ponder the meaning and value of these and other traditional observances. This idea of just fasting one day a year for the forgiveness of my sins raised perplexing questions in my heart and mind. How could I fast just one day a year and the rest of the year do whatever I wished? And then the question of forgiveness began to loom greater and greater as time passed and I progressed into areas of life that I inherently knew were not pleasing to God.

I graduated from high school at the age of 16 (almost 17) and went on to college, becoming fascinated by a lifestyle that would eventually shape all of my activities during that period: the life of wine, women, and song. Rock music and my large collection of albums and tapes became a kind of inner haven as the rock musicians seemed to strike chords deep within my soul. I was also lured by the beauty of women in different girlfriends and pictures, all the time trying to keep things hidden from my parents.

I recall one day noticing a button on a girl's jacket that stated, "Sin now, pray later." The impact of that statement I will never forget, because I thought, "That's me!" My religious upbringing was still there, buried deep under outer layers of sin. I still feared God, and in retrospect, I believe that by his Holy Spirit the button on that rebellious girl's jacket was used gently by God to convict me of my sin.

I graduated from college in 1985 at the age of 21. In May of 1986, I was up in the late hours of the evening watching television (as was my habit then) when I heard a slight rumbling sound outside. I went to our seventh-floor apartment window and stuck my head out but saw nothing. A few moments later, the strange noise outside occurred again. I went over to the window once more but saw nothing in the sky... And then suddenly a thought crossed my mind.... "This is it! The Christians were right! JESUS IS COMING BACK, and it's tonight!!" For a few seconds, my eyes were riveted to the sky as I waited for the horses to appear through the nighttime clouds and for this Jesus to return as I knew the Christians said he would do one day.

I'd listened to TV evangelists growing up, and obviously something had stuck with me. The Lord obviously did not part the clouds that night, but His Spirit DID begin to penetrate through my clouded heart. I suddenly realized that night how afraid I was of dying (because I knew that I was a sinner), and I told God that I would give up things that I knew were wrong. The fear eased, but...

Forgiveness. How does one really get it? That was my question. Deep down I knew there had to be something more than just one day of fasting a year to secure forgiveness, but what was it? Somehow the TV evangelists had impressed me with the fact that forgiveness and Jesus went together, and that week I was very passionately driven to understand how it all worked. There was no putting this off any longer. As the girl's button had said, "Sin now, pray later," but now I knew for certain that God had not promised me that there would be a 'later'. I sought out how to be forgiven with all my heart. The synagogue had never spoken clearly of any afterlife, and I didn't want to walk into the foreign territory of a church since I was Jewish! But I remembered an organization I'd heard of named Jews for Jesus! Obviously there were other people who are Jewish and believe in Jesus...

I called their offices and told the man on the other end that, basically, I wanted to be saved. He offered to meet me downtown. When we met, he answered some of my questions and gave me some good Bible literature to read. One of the pieces included the sinner's prayer, and I think I prayed it on the train while returning home. I also called "The 700 Club" and prayed with a phone counselor who assured me I was saved and heaven-bound.

My behavior changed drastically after that, but needless to say, my family was not pleased with me breaking up with my girlfriend, breaking all my rock albums, etc... I was ushered in to see our family rabbi, a family counselor, and two trained anti-missionaries. But even with all their words throwing me into confusion, God still had His hand on me. One Friday, at a Shabbat Messianic service, I heard a tremendous message by a Jewish believer named J'han Moskowitz. God used that message and the man mightily in my life, and that night all my doubts and fears literally melted away. I knew for a fact that Jesus was indeed the Jewish Messiah, and I responded during the invitation / rededication.

I began reading all that I could about the Lord and the Bible. The messianic prophecies in the Jewish scriptures (like Isaiah 53, Daniel 9:24-26, etc.) pointed to Yeshua (Jesus) so clearly! Each day I grew closer to Him, and eventually I was asked to leave my family's apartment. It worked out for the best, however... I was able to move in with another Jewish believer and began to read the scriptures like never before - without fear of having my Bible confiscated this time (like my mom used to do.)

Since then, the Lord has done marvelous things. A few years ago my mom came to faith herself (weakly, but she is there, I believe. She even saw Yeshua with her while in the hospital!) I thank God for all that He has done in my life these almost 40 years now! I look forward to the day when I will meet my Messiah face to face.

<u>Rock of Israel Ministries</u> is a Messianic Jewish
ministry that wishes to proclaim Jesus as Messiah to
the Jewish people. We also wish to teach the church
the Jewish roots of their faith.

For more books and Judiaca – visit our website or call
our main office in Ohio.

We have a free email newsletter that comes out
monthly. There is also a printed newsletter that comes
out semi-annually. Just send us a request, and you
will receive it at no charge.

Doug (and others at the Rock of Israel) are also
available to teach in your church or congregation. We
travel all over.

For more information, contact us.

Rock of Israel Ministries
P.O. Box 18038
Fairfield, OH 45018
513-874-2566
www.rockofisrael.org
Email: info@rockofisrael.org

Made in the USA
Columbia, SC
27 May 2025

58553448R00061